# SELF-DESTRUCTION

**Library of Congress Cataloging-in-Publications Data**

Moriarty, Laura.
Self-destruction / Laura Moriarty
p. cm.
ISBN 0-942996-51-8 (acid-free paper)
I. Title

PS3563.O871635S45 2004
811'.54--dc22

2004044772



The Post-Apollo Press
35 Marie Street
Sausalito, California 94965

Cover photo and book design by Simone Fattal
Cover design by Simone Fattal and Kathleen Wilkinson

*Printed in the United States of America on acid-free paper.*

Laura Moriarty

# SELF-DESTRUCTION

THE POST-APOLLO PRESS

By the Same Author

*Nude Memoir,* Krupskaya, 2000.

*Duse,* reprinted by Paradigm Press, 2000; originally published by Coincidence Press, 1987.

*Cunning,* Spuyten Duyvil, 1999

*The Case,* O Books, 1998.

*Spicer's City,* Poetry New York, 1998

*Symmetry,* Avec Books, 1996.

*L'Archiviste,* Zasterle Press, 1991.

*Rondeaux,* Roof Books, 1990.

*like roads,* Kelsey St. Press, 1990.

*Persia.* Chance Additions, 1984. Poetry Center Book Award winner.

*Two Cross Seizings,* Sombre Reptiles, 1980.

# SELF-
# DESTRUCTION

Acknowledgements

The author wishes to thank Lee Chapman for publishing a selection of this work in *First Intensity,* No. 19, 2004.

Contents

"Let me sing you// two yous A shred"

Taylor Brady, *Microclimates*

# My Disappearance

"In its cruelty the mind demands two contradictory things: to hear itself and to escape itself...But even then the mind is vigilant, and begins to see the shadow of its theatrical self."

Brent Cunningham, *Bird & Forest*

# Gone Again

Texture of stucco
Regarder of sounds (listener)
"reaching back in the night to grope for a pillow"
Finding you are not home
"not yet at the edge"
For it is *who* that appears and disappears
"You are also like this [but] who could not be you?"
When bombs fall
The disappearance is adorned
Momentum
Terror
Josephine
*My Disappearance*
The moon today
Not yet gone

## Convention

Not unlike the moon. Eyes open all the time. When we talk we sound the same for a while and then depart. We meet like conventioneers. I trade a definition of myself for a thousand years of history. Random House. Against the tempo. Back through the aisles unable to find where we are and then finding it. Finally the walls simply open and we walk out into the dusk. I had no idea what would happen. Even so I was wrong. We were wrong in our expectations.

## First Song

Tell me to sing
A series to serenade to calm
To clarify to drizzle
Walk go along to the ocean
Without light with light to the sea
You were with me in hell
It wasn't like hell
We were under the sea
The same as love you were/are
Tell me to embrace you
Carry you off two or three ways
How many in this song
How many times going
Gone by boat to the sea
More sacred to us than something
Tell me to hold you

## First Entry

I'll go wherever you want me to go. What was said. What was sung. A pure lie. Like a door in my forehead, as before in my chest. The corridors of that movement. Blurry radio sound early in the morning. What I do to keep it going. He wakes up again with nothing. This is what he prefers. He likes the sense of things collapsing around him. I tell him it's not over.

## No Date

Not one place or the other. Carefully. Two cities by the water. Two of us. One among islands. Having left off as myself. Left behind. Changed something. As perhaps confidence in existing. Panic. A new name. A new instrument. Whose questioning and whose perseverance also leaves off. Here at the table as if in the hotel again. The return. The sound in us when we play. Too much of something.

# First Dream

First dream against walls
The scene pressed into unsaid
But possible as pictured without
Control as with dream the scale
Large the scene clear of will
Of what disturbs you
*My question*
In the courtyard the hotel statue
The wings of it poised
Too much singing
To yourself, myself
Conventional fountain but dry
Agreement also silent

## Fate/Song Form

Blameless this claim
That I or you

Do nothing no one
Knows where you are

Animal or minimal
Second the seconds passed

Allowed by you or that I
Would have

Slowly around us the field
Did you hear me?

With clarity as if not
Needing it to be real

## A Letter

Life not releasing (unfolding)
Me letting go
The world not escaping (me)
The street this one long
Arrives but not
Shelter I
Into the light of day
Fields, mountains anywhere
Not catching myself
Thirst
But soaked in
Not rain but sky
Blue, I don't resist
Your heaven your blue I
Distance (tomorrow)
Your insistence
I am made by you
Backward
Looking back
Looking forward to

## Thief in Your Voice

Give me (reaching)
This first enough
The open door
When the court brings itself
As if waking to order
Because you counted
Recounted to the police
Incarcerated (incorporated)
Myself found
The cell door closed
No one knocks or knows
Not even the thief
No one appears
Who is not a thief
Opens (is open to) a window
Shaft of light
Like a gardener or door
Seizes the light (you)
Not knowing that she (I) gives herself

And where am I you say that I am
Not a gardener in a garden
But a thief
In a town with no people
With closed doors
Who accounts for the absence

Of the thief who appears
Saying Take care my love
Take care of my love

And where am I that I am
A thief in this place
Where I am here with no one
In this garden

## Place

This ache
Ageless
Longing
Age this

Place
Transit
Young age
Aching is

Age
Scene of our
Place our
Trance

This change
Transitive
Placeless
Age of

## Meeting

He let go of me
What no one turns
Returns like a wheel (embarks)
Revisits remains

All the sugar in the world
Cafe china fantasy of white not
Leaving here not stopped
A juke box starts

The way back
Now this act
A short song
The road tangled

Apostasy to take
Give oneself up to
One who sings
Has already has left

Sleepy now not
Understanding night
Without sleep
All that is wanted

A phrase away
Is late the street wakes

He takes himself
Not meeting

# Tin Box

Heart with nails
No words
Car starting
The play

Lime and mint
*Ciudad*
Come here for this
Lit from within

Homage á  Jack
His traveling name
Address floating
Paper trembling wings

Fans in this heat
"That was all he could do"
Car start repetition
The dead team Us

Many songs end to end convince us to speak. The red pools like a sea in the courtyards of the city. We land there. The fans circle like buzzards. We lay still. Open also unfolded. Of paper speaking when there was nothing else. The reliquary we carry.

## Meeting

Any city
Not this city
To return to repeat
To drink with him (you)

Landing in the wrong
Army in the city haze
What have I done?
Small arms fire

This time threatens
Unreal again birds
From the garden mixed
With our sounds

## No Date

Temporary like the moon or the effect of medicine. There is a black market in these moons. They are not anxious or panicked but full and round. Unable to stop. Stop laughing. Stop singing. Finally. Eat. Today's hunger makes us dizzy. Too much hunger. There is too much hunger today. Not enough moon. You are not in it. My mind. Our work. The war.

## Second Event

Rough green song
That something was
Oneself that state
Seemed unprepared
Or is

Traditional event
Or still ancient
Which was audible
A sudden display
Like rain over

Also suddenly (another place)
Challenged my papers
Not knowing
I was there

## Earth Forgotten

Stucco to terracotta

In cameo half sky

From one direction the town

Size unclear the eyes also

Too long gone

The constant misremembered

Beginning of time

Depersonalized but okay

*Destination Moon*

Protagonist cratered and pale

Seeks inaccurate revenge

Travels by thinking

## August 1

The moon comes apart over a different place. Hopelessly it is the only constant. Also the job. Destination management. Barking dog. A woman falls in the street. Later she falls again. Injures herself. I come back carrying my bag in my arms like a dog. Don't get up.

## Stupid Moon

Stupid moon
Unfortunate creature in it

Voice like a whistle
Source of rumors

Used me like a radio
Innuendo of success left

They call it the clap
When after something

A dose men say
That said

My name for you
Not written here

Sleeps among the nerves of the spine. A symptomatic rage. By the time you read this. Not dose but does. Does he know?

## Paid In Full

Handing over (handed)
Surrender
Wind inside
Being in thought
Circular singular
Narcotic

Seeing into
Delivery
Giving up quickly
As through a lens
Circular thick
Leafy

Having none
To get drunk
Hand over
Sticky with
Enough
Circular
Overcome

## Without Me

Hotel window stars
Fixed there
Not mad or sad
Clear glass frame
Hills in the houses
Distance
(The forgetting of what is between us is
hidden in your mind.)
Not like eyes unlike also
Planets arranged
Tray of unmatched things

# The Phrase Identical

To itself. The convention of my being. The convention of being. Everything is new. Before being for a while anywhere. Trying to get. Transferred. Setting limits to this new. Prescription. Place. Falling back on the habits of my companion. But is that me? Hold breath to avoid spending air.

## In the Lobby

Of what
Distinction unclear

The elevated
Instrumental (or dissent)

Reading at last
Against sense

With attention
But without witness

Existing
Only here

"Live" music
All I hear

All day
Morning just

Waiting waking
Unready

With and without
The "and" search

Leads back
Empty tables

Empty tables and chairs
Failed translation

Living memorial
"And" again

## The War

My neighbor is afraid of spiders. We aren't really neighbors. We are people who talk about the war. There is little to say. The revenge is familiar. Familial. There is an Imperium recreating and organizing itself. There are people on TV in our neighborhood. Not wanting to move. Looking everywhere for a place to stop. My neighbor is not among them. He is here. There is an Imperium. He and I find we are covered by its will. We return to our rooms. An early state of desire. Substitute lover for neighbor. No desire. No speech.

## The Force Of

The sea after us, your terrors
Overextended out into
Possible though limited activity
The chase
The severe coastline visible
Trail up into the cliff thick with
Panorama the wind up
The ship of another country
In the distance
I won't I say you say
I will make you

# Tranquility

Delimited by asterisk
The second storm and quotes
From the perspective
Of a backward purchase
Almost June

Weather deteriorating
Escape to a tranquil sea
Landing like the moon
The moon book
The old trip

Divided and put out
The equipment we had
A traveling problem revisited
Of too much movement
But did it happen?

# Time-line

An unraveling. No argument. There is almost no time but the afternoon never ends. He stays with it. The news from there. The nationality. The irrationality In a crowd staring back knowing. I have my usual fear. And still no time has passed. People in a room I know. The worst thing. Room for negotiation. His hair that way.

The language was strange
Not loving him more than anyone else
I appear in her journal

Later the language was strange of the women near me. There was no concentration in my listening. Was it Latinate? Were they young or old?

I find I don't love him more than anyone else. No stories exist about him in my head. There is no indifference. We are not chaste today. But have agreed to nothing. He doesn't seem to exist any more than I do.

The question concerns leaving off. Identity continues. This identity is only as long as or ends even before we do. This does. Not like grammar.

The break in my need for "medication" is established by the discontinuity in the time-line. Why even call it that?

## False Moon Waltz

View from inside
One planet to another
Planet giants barely there
Come from here The news

Where the moon is now
Looking down from the moon
Tranquility Base an imagined place
The breath from that event

Take me away from the moon
Exhausted by this elaborate stage
Pretending to be here every day
Where I am. How do I know?

# Dear Fate

To the fates in a circle
Because memory
An "other than" result
This letter also
The same event
A fresh pen
And parameters
Gift of my interlocutor

Calm all the hours
"I am, mistress, unable to lie"
The truth is this fate
But are you mine?
The trip planned in a previous life
Overtaken now
Reading matter in advance
The map's haphazard mileage
The moon's curve
And still not there
"I wait on your pleasure"
The weather is worse

Being without relation with regard
To this fate meaning the present
In an oddly named town
In a Great Basin

From a book by someone else
"I am master now"

Six towers partially destroyed
Before going underground
In another city
Before leaving you there

## Song As Example

Disconsolate
Pleasure-loving

Disarranged
Inhabited mass

Animals
Feeling of life

Indifferent languor
Self-sufficient

Apropos of nothing
By their example

Moss hanging
Shaded clings

Grave bent
Without looking

Duration
(Laughed)

Invincible
Invisible

## Add Date

It was our fate to laugh a lot during our meetings. He was hard to know. Anything could be said. Blind with love. His genius was like his virginity. A dye soaking through him. I worried he would become a social pariah. We both had jobs. He never traveled.

Begin he said
But we don't
The place we made of our
City together
The beginning he began (to himself)
To arrive continuously together (he said)
We live in different worlds
Our towns concurrent with
Our meetings are
Stated as such or inasmuch
I needn't have thought
I needn't have known
Didn't know

# The Lunar Convention

The convent in which daughters once languished. The convention. A lavish production of a novel. A biography of a poet. His way to kill time. An organizational method. "Le methode" meant sex to him. Fated child. He is bright. He plays brightly. The sound fills us with disquiet.

Words are set to music soothing to the reader. The writer is surprised to be taken in this way. "The Singing Moon" is an increasingly rare instance of melody holding its own with harmony and rhythm.

The two moons of Mars rise in relation to Mars and each other. Our moon is framed by a branch of oak. The moon, rhymed with "soon" evokes the "still and bright" of a previous stanza in time. When the moon rhymes it is the convention of the moon. The lunar convention applies equally to the actual satellite. That both moon and rhyme are conventional is a relief. It is the relief that suggests a face, an expression. Belief. The moon's expression is inexact, inaccurate. But it is the same inaccuracy we have come to know. We come back to it. Together we regard the moon. Confident of our existence. Guarded about the conventionality of the moon.

## Sing Song

To mess up one's hair or life
To squander to spend to throw off course

To tear apart farewell dismissal
In spite of to pour to empty out

Tumble down unwanted despair
Expensive unnoticed

To be free from doing
Grand hotel oneself installed

The rest before the sound

## My Passing

My past is unrecorded
My passing was discontinued disconcerted

Deserted there in that place
A confidential situation

The truth for you
For a change wanting to go

A tantrum of cooperation
As if "I" was alone

Tense jumbled storm broken
Too soon back without

Questions or objections
Without doubt

## Sounded while reading

Doves not owls
Delacroix with Byron

Becomes a version
Of a feather with the noble

Posture broken famously
By nature and fate

Is there a difference?
As you hear them quietly

Under the skin
Exotic to themselves

Out late until morning
Early mixed

Concupiscent as doves
After the flight

Nothing but to lie
Unidentified

## Dawn (No Fate)

But fate is only speaking
Prophecy in reverse explained
She merrily in the situation
Doubly inappropriate

Lace things hung to dry
Luggage open
The split with the past

Nemesis is equilibrium the future
Not there every day
Present tense blank drawn
Fits of responsibility
In the form of letters
Ones that were used against
Expression

Thick coffee too strong
Things here sweet Too much work
I don't miss you
I can't know this

## Duration

It was the right location but ten years too soon. The coming change in the neighborhood evident but not actual. Like a cartoon wizard living backwards. I had missed you. Missed your time entirely. There was a decade to go. Deaths. Children.

Half-asleep mocking birds and self. Half-remembered magpies from somewhere else. Independent contractor. A sum equals a certain interval. Close to the ground. Close to the chest. Restraint is possible. But within it a measured sequence is planned and occurs. The voice that produces the duration is not mine.

# Moon after morning after

Wells poisoned in the news
Double charge for medicine
Useless now
Refilled too soon

Disappearing moon
The need to drink from the well
Delacroix's Byron (You are)
Ruined watercolor allegory

A country as a woman
I to you
Dissolve like chemicals
Used up like them

## Convention

Entry. Overcast inside. The leaves in the local wind.

It is understood what you are. Everyone together in one place. I am. Server and served. Vendor and vended. Exhausted. Extended. Misplaced. Missent. Undersigned. Undernamed. Artificially happy. Vented. Exitless. Suspended in conventional air.

## From the Map

Related to me
This Empire

Landlocked
"My" people left

Europe desperate ending up
Somewhere cold or here hot

No one alive remembers
No one dead

Only on paper
My antecedents

Mental landscape
Where never

## Convention

It is understood that lovers desire or stand for or physically possess each other or want to. Both lovers must know of the relationship and define it as such. Or at least one of them must know and want the other. Instances of stalking or obsession are tiresome, though famous lovers might fall into this category. But we (you) don't. In our world obsessive love is either a crime against personal freedom or a crime against a child. But we are not children.

Our relationship is perfect. Profound but unemotional, ephemeral, undemanding, passionate but asexual. We are like two words separated by a period. Attached to different sentences but following each other. A sequence. A phrase. We are a logic, an explanation.

You suspect me of irony, of writing a love letter. I am not. Innocent or otherwise. My silence and disappearance are not my fault. This is a breakthrough for both of us, especially you. For me it is a new virginity, true only of this situation. An intactness that surrounds us (each) like a translucent gauze. It allows us to writhe and stretch while retaining the sense of being covered. Of being almost unborn. But again only to each other. It is typical of us that you will not read this and in what sense can "I" be said to have written it? You of all people know that my identity is precarious. My attachment to it almost nonexistent (like my virginity). Like this war.

## Missing

I don't miss my friends
Who have become unknown to me
The truth can't be communicated
The war keeps us in touch

From one direction only the sky
Letters not about love
Delivered randomly people die
They watch themselves as they fall

Nothing misses us
Opened like a letter
Already before it happens
I won't know

## Pessoa

Airborne again "I" scream
Into the limited air where
Out into the aisle a head

Mine held hard with pain
The calm of being in movement
Forward in time but backward in fate

Morning milky nightgown sky
Steam everywhere sleep but (with pain)
Undecided. No desire. No argument.

Pessoa: To do something is to rest
The ticket in this book.
No one but you your

Monogamy
His vampire sensibility.
He pages through the score

Monotonously the plane.
The world the wind. The word.
Himself to himself.

## Keeping Time

Wrought holler
Heat morning late lilac
Lighter than the sky
Ghost steps behind
Invisible ramparts
Up from the river
Lets out into
Moist window
The participant changes
What changes
Who forgets time

## Hot Date

... envy of reality. My air. My smoke. Is there any news? Am I back? The open space of the square stops. Your sensibility causes me to ache. The Irish in the French Quarter. I have forgotten to be myself. Sudden drop in temperature. The clouds and what are those winged things?

Direct sun at the grave. Air teeming. "Imaginary semen in electric current." Too far in the heat. The contortionist waves from the balcony. Otherwise known as me. The street heats up again. Another square ahead. Another opening.

## Sycorax Inside

Blood of arrival racing
Wood cunted between breasts

Arriving to repeat arriving
Between cities hot at this

Cool sheets and sky (Césaire)
"the blue dog of metamorphosis"

Mental Traveler between
Arrivals I'm sorry I

Couldn't wait to arrive
Trunk along with chest (thorax)

Exhausted the walls along side
Winged vermin gilded

Wet steps fluctuate
Hot to cold to

Square of constant
Lightning from the bed

Out of order
Storm breaks again

No events but in time
The edge of the flood

Ceding to sleep anything
Permeable the screen

Like a sieve the rain
Not touching me

## Any Day

"Any year starts as a literal translation."
Alan Halsey, *Auto Dada Cafe*

Accoutrements of mind fully
Iron stairs the shaky stance

Of tenants identified as guests
Of themselves late at work still

I pay myself to be here
"Important things about to happen"

But which of these is it? The books
Cooked in this light the collected

Books arrive with your order
The maps include every detail

Brightness also hot and here
Dry but wet there

A paragraph per location biscuits
Promised every morning homemade

Jam but made there
In a state of constant replacement

She called. That was the echo.
Displacement in columns like numbers

Associated with gender but literal
I never get anywhere complaint

Translation project on-going
There were no exceptions to his love

## Josephine

Fine
Affinity

Sign of

Seraphic
Phatic or
Fate

Italic

Plant or
Gesture
Serene
Final

Pine

## Recorded Sound

Hotel home
Several days away
Forget I don't live
In my room
With a man
With fever
From a distance
The driver delivers me
His world
Hot with
History
Outside air
Or which place is here
A man by his landscape
Compiled from notes
A woman
A man was home
Whose excessive
Improvisation
He climbs the stairs
So that later
*Played me*
Born there
In that hotel
Downtown

## Fallen For

Some cheap guy
In satin
On your street

Red plush
With lines
Recognizable as

Making a mask
With its feathers
Unnecessary

Undead as
We meet in sleep
Everyone here

## Letter

Decadence is what we have. The slightest gesture. As a sort of weeping in place. Your collection of junk of the same color. How I added to it. Where it's always a holiday. In some anguish but not yet. Things in stone in this town. Missed your act. I can't keep those hours now. Or know what you sing. What you know.

## My Dance

The dance I do for you
The form outside
Your distracted eyes as
The demonstration
Arms raised hair loosened
But inclusive
Holds and opens in your hands
Sees you later still
Arguing as we resume
In costume
Our discussion with other dancers
Our definition
Of practice is departure
My definition
Only during this transaction
Of a beautiful man

# Interval

The hotel will keep these
Famous last words
Terrible ephemeral

Lovely silence
Passes all time
My knowledge of this (him)

Crushed together
Like silk things
On the road

All the time
The movie in the morning
The only light

## Triangulation

Widowed moon
Daily news diary
False parallels

Hotel pen
The northern plain
Surrounding wind

Chairs and lake
Hotel sweat
Courtyard door

Leafstorm
Time of:
Another state

## Ceasura

Back to the moon
Its pyramids
Its phases
Phrases
Lyric entity
The instability of the moon
Truncates until
The conventional the convention
Floor staring up from
The sea of eyes
Notebook ticket debris
Stationary but falling
Rain near the sea
Start of night
Stark stares
As when the sun

## My God

About dawn another
Woman yelling hotel
Outside the double

Window door
Sounded like a siren
Or musical saw

A dark taste the haze
Asleep beside me
Notebook

Oak table chair
Chest painted strange
Gods evoked

## My Name

My name but changeable
Fan spinning above my head
A house of water
Something cool

An empty field and palms
My life is only this
Fountain not a shrine
But fully

He claims but I don't know
The words simply or only
Melody was that surprise
Falling in

Falling in with us he called
Me as a single note
A glass door closed and bolted
But not before

## The Phrase In Time

The phrase is open. Complete. Incomplete in its manipulation of time. A long traveling and arrival into possibility. Normal pain. Let down. Picking up at the end, it repeats. An accusation is incomplete or is understood. A complaint or description. The sense of scale picks up at the end. It opens and repeats.

What city did I see that movie in? Not for the first or last time but many times down the road. A question of being caught in time. Each time. A noun phrase. Vulnerable to change. Having changed artificially. Creating a new unnatural symmetry, a chemical seeks itself in a living system. Unspecific. A bird or flower. Specific. Me or you. In this case me. Alone in this room. Compartmentalized but open. Out there. On the street or on the floor. Let me tell you about the deal.

The fan in the mirror framed in tin. A woman swims in the courtyard pool. Hidden by bougainvillea. Birds of paradise and lemons. A man speaks softly next door. Explaining. Another voice intervenes, starting again, from the top. From the window. Walls yellow. Guests in silhouette. Broken English. Breaking it again.

Comforter coiled on the bed. Comfortless. Salmon pink and blue. The pattern suggest a Navajo blanket or Turkish kilim. Oneself as form. These courtyards. Lavish fountains in this canyon. Manmade landscape. Meaning dawn or fate. Lemon trees. Thick with. An arrangement in tin. In time.

Hotel television. Won't mute. Artificial continuity. Continuous longing. Silence. The frame repeats. The tin incised in dented whorls. White negligee. Yellow kimono. Nothing can be done. An issue of scale. Connectedness. Theme. Unclear how high this mountain behind us. Or how far back down. We can only say the time.

Not duck but crow. A reflection or sound. Where would a duck go in this desert? Where have you gone? The crows look like gods. Dust. This is not about love. But about sound. This is a great shopping town. Where would you go?

Handmade. Medicated. I offer my hand to the manikin. Recorded sound. Recorded bells. Made of time. Ink on silk. A rough night followed by a hot dawn. Resonance. Between us. We've lived in every state. In every time. The figure is like a face. Recognition. There is no echo. The sound stays inside.

Limits. The tin. A recorded car starts. Giving onto a percussive story which is smooth but abrupt. The mirror pools inside the tin. Is it a physical or electronic silence? What about the ducks? A moving sound. Mockingbird framed in blue. A boom box goes by. The listener carries it forward. Various mechanisms stop it. The sound follows. It leaves you flat. Gives over.

Once in a while there is a sense of scale. A simple descent. A pace. Interval and repetition. I look for you looking for the event.

Breathless and then breathing intent into the next thing. Silence in that moment expands indefinitely. Adjectivally. Modified by a person or a place. By a thing. By nothing. She translates as she sings.

Her thoughtful intonation is not a style but an exposition. It occupies her. Narrative exists as if in another world. It is an ordinary day. An interval. A Tuesday. You are named for a deity. Each animal in its niche. The gold frame. She sells them to you. I remind myself. She is not me. She is not fucking me.

Gone off somewhere. There is a soundtrack in another time. An amplified theme in a public setting. People hover like angels. Death is present in a series of endings. Theaters open onto each other. The logic is flawless. You could build a city with it. A desert community. Crows appear with the first heat.

I run that movie in my head. I don't need to buy it. Back in the cool room. Note to read Spicer on oranges. Lemons vivid. The unnaturally early dusk begins with the sun behind the mountain. Spanish from the street. Tin framed in time. Belief. I thought I took it. I found I left it behind.

There are ducks. Thousands of ducks in the Salton Sea. An ocean troubled by limits. A remnant. Night has already started in this valley. In this room. A canyon in warm shadow. Yellow oak. Yellow and green palm. A aureole of salt around the sea.

*Madrugada.* The word isolated like the mountains in this desert. An island ecology. An assertion of scale when storms from the coast finally reach us. The edges of them like music overheard. No subject. No consistency.

We are at a crossroads from which numbers rise in either direction. The changes in scale constitute an accusation. It is a question of the business plan. Relentless pursuit. Our intimacy. That one book. Map with no details. The return of heat with the return of day. Violet habitat. Many kinds of sand.

The sound of the weather. First the breath of the singer. Her voice begins rough and broadens quietly. Flat and then sweet. Like rain. There is a question but no complaint. No point but an invasive knowledge. A context. The words are familiar. They are the usual words. Each next one unsurprising. Though taken as they are heard, there is departure. An expected repetition. Nothing to do with fate but in form. A conversation. Many words and then music.

Cross country. Scrambling up rock. Cactus. Broken glass trail. An alteration in minutes. Hours. A short distance but vertical. Looking back at what climbed and descended. Scaled. Bells again from far below. I am aware that I am falling. Fallen. Sand or ground. Sandstone. Creosote. Abandoned stairs. Incipient meteor shower overhead. Ancient backyard. Red tiles remain all that is left of the floor. Detached fireplace. Stairs ending. This is not a trail.

Companion. Small desert coyote in the diorama. Holes in the dust. This mountain is full of holes. Also logic. Song as example. Creatures flash past the sun. Interrupt its light. People. He follows me. He imagines a war in which the people lose. Our empire's music retains the sadness of its victims. Lady. He says. The trail is by the big juniper. Do you want me to take you there? What do you want?

Walled courtyard. Dusk. The history of oranges. Raccoons in the pool. The familiar clarity of the local air. Distance between plants in the desert. Flesh on TV. The best place for implants. The distance between us. Between them. Real estate. Fountain and pool. Terra cotta. Arch.

Incessant water sound. Florentine stars painted on the mask in the bathroom. Your face here. A scrap of handwriting by a dead woman in a borrowed book. The music becomes thoughtful. The suitcase is open on the bed.

Gradients of heat. Harvesting the wind. The morning travels north.

## One of These Days

Josephine. Only not long. Introduction. We are introduced. Again. Yet we don't come to know each other. A costume. An association. A convention. I am. She is. A saying. A clay cup. Negligee. Negligent. A phrase.

The appearance of trouble. The notebooks become infested on the trip. A sort of powder. Put them in plastic. They bleed. She is identified. Dreams the autopsy. The nature of being already unalive. Not dead. Half-life. Or end. The phrase as part of itself. Insects from there. Jointed. From then.

Humming. Abrupt stop. Continuation of the phrase in time. Landing. Continuation of the breath. Phrases from another language. Incomplete translation. Decorative mask. The skull in my skin. Hotel complex. She doesn't sound awake.

I am missing. Mishka. Power failing. Voice falters. He also fades. His famous alterity. Sings quiet. Smoke surrounds his face. He lets himself go in words. She stays sane. More or less. Her letters are detached. Medicated. Mediated. Additional titles arrive. She arrives. Added to the mix.

Survival. The only question. The war. Extension. Extensions. Identical with the map or schedule. *National Geographic.* Unquestioned. In exile. The translation begins where the empire leaves off. She can't personalize because she isn't a person. A continent. Or globe. Breakthrough. Breakdown. New medicine.

# Choir

Drowned out by the wind
"In a twinkling"
The accompaniment
A boy sings

Before you were born
The moon unplanned
A chemical impression
A dust storm

Beyond his years
High wind
High end of the scale
Each page a moon

Don't sing he sang
From the same plane
The horizon
Or compromise

## Unexplored

Traveler's globe
Revolutionary calendar
Humboldt current

The problem of another universe. Sea within a sea. I took that pleasure. Once. A single event. Now many. Explored. Exploded but unexplored. Named for a man. Or for you. Antique heaven. Portable. Cool to the touch.

Uncontained sound
No one to hear
Nothing

## Visible Because

Vertical light
Among buildings
Polished brass
Deal

Color of air
Two per square
*Fleur de lys*
Business where

Overnight accumulation
Unmelted day
Where you are
Divided by the sun

Opened and pulled up
Blind
Not able to say
When

## Time After Time

The medicine has left me. Your word for that repetition. Don't repeat yourself. The breath in your chest. Exposed. Surprised at this age. This time. You said, "This time come back." One from the past. Or not quite. Not the past. Not the present. There are those who have a sense of that time. I hate them.

Recorded birdsong. Movie music. Always dawn. Tuesday again. Third day. I am sorry I wasn't thinking when we spoke. An instrumental version of the same song. The effect of beauty on you. Me watching.

# The Other Thing

"Music not separate from history" Anthony Braxton

Crossing the street against the wind
He is against themes or me having them

I repeat he repeats the repetition
The piano plays itself in the lobby

He sleeps in my lap
The music laps around us in the lobby

He wakes up preparing to speak
I look down at the sound

## View From

Organized water
Lake

Hotel literature
Pain where

Half moon
Michigan Avenue Bridge

Organized crime
Hard time

Pitched
Lower than

Eyes can
Organized sound

Out of town
Eyes can see

## Lines of Palm

Between the wall and the plane
The plane and the stairs
The corridor is cold

Lines of palm on the horizon
Back up into the air
Facing down into the world

Unable to move or breathe
Superfluous presence or shut down
Inaudible over the roar

Area along the river between the river
And the wall below the bridge and fountain
In the middle of town

## To See To Be

Being only a function of the medicine. My heart like birds. Keeping my head in one place with an effort. To see to write. Startled by room service. Hot sky. Not bright.

Night comes with her. Side effects. Birds land in trees to sleep already heavy with birds. This walking among houses like stage sets. He sees us in the yard of oak and pecan. I cry because of the cedar.

## Arrival

Parking lot bare trees dawn
A long time and then later
Indistinctly seen simply filled
The same sky also plain

Abandoned between times
She couldn't come back
A small moon from the window
I see that now

## Fountain

But I don't see how
To avoid recorded bells
At a predicted interval
Admittedly long

Oak and limestone material
For his presentation
Flowers and dolls but not
Ironic in his movement

Around the room like puppets
Rows of us like a choir
A procession of static from the church
Electronic time-based incidents

The sacristy was a shower
There was an acre of lawn
Remembered water in sheets
The fountain a maze

## My Time

Overvoice
Time zone figures
Infinite regress
Patterns of loss
Squared rug corridor
Stretches into
Unmedicated delay

A voice trained to speak. It is all you can say. This is not the world. You act as if the voice is in my head.

Your self-conscious representation of the end of time allows you to follow my voice with an argument. There is a struggle. You are surprised by the instrumentation – by the voice. The new music sounds old to you. Is old. Meanwhile we try to forget the similarity of every building in town. The same stone. The same stars. The time.

It becomes clear we are the only ones in the terminal. Everything closes. We fly up into the rain. We land in the rain. I leave myself there. Eyes red. I listen to my voice. Bags to the side. Sit in a strange position as in a hotel but more open. As if at home. Traveling through the rain. Not gone. Not home. The windows hot with breath. You realize you are alone with me. With the voice. Going but not knowing.

## Protocol

Love by love qualified
The new criminal class
Music from the war
Negative impact on biological diversity
Strange plan
Sleep left behind
Statistics trains sirens
A row of stones
He speaks from the book
But his tone is sweet

Come dance with me
The war opens
"I've got to be," he said "next"
Later from the train window
Double speech
Rain and birdsong
On the front line
Sings himself into place
The resulting line item
Don't leave me all alone

## For the Birds

I concentrate on the radio in the afternoon during pain. During rain. They follow me into space. The machine breaks open to reveal our conversation. Call letters. Graphic love. We are not from the same time but the trajectory reaches down our throats and into our hearts. As frightening as the landscape was as it took itself apart, it was worse to wait. The birds at dawn. The hotel was not responsible.

## My Dream

We arrive together
My disgrace
Demand that I

For a night
A small garden
Or abyss

Future explicit
In that house
The likes of you

## Deadline

We stop before running across. Watching the light. Talk including silence. The road trip. More work. The forest is incidental. Appointed time. Just getting started thunderstorm. You and I are supporters of each other. We work together. A robot plays the music. The others are lost.

To desert each other. Be sublime. Break up. Resist be reconciled. Cry out to proclaim in the meeting. Notes. Instead of speech he arranges for what happens to seem real. We pretend to believe him. The light changes again. Dusk. Still working. Night the same. Pay back agenda. Play back in my head. We do believe him. Mechanical memory. The robot in my heart.

Tempo. Temporal meaning storm. The original people in the project. Camped out in some desperation. Ourselves to be delivered.

As if God had left. A system meltdown. Because of the way he said his "I's" and by the lack of medicine. The next cut. Like a holy card or radio broadcast. Inexact. Edged in gold, we made our voices into instruments. The word of God in music. The money. We positioned ourselves to receive the maximum remuneration. Like an echo. But it wasn't like that. We arrived early throwing everything down. Behind the hotel bar. Behind the piano. Notes taken. Pain gone.

# The Second You

"I love me for I *am* the public."

John Wilkinson, *The Speaking Twins*

## The Second You

We go on a little
After the new
The second you see me
To exist we stop

I am already you complain
All your silence is mine
The form of your mind
Mine to lose

Mine to have lost
The named phases
Gravity like grief holds
Nothing like the moon

# Cryptophasia

Our language is not the only thing keeping us apart. The leaves are blinding in the morning. I didn't understand it to be physical but it was. We are. Information. Doubles. Our attachment to small talk means the world to me. He is telling his own story, making it up with chance input from the word and the world. He is a con artist. He is lost in his work. The leaves are white in the sun dating from before the war. Before either of us was born. But now we are born.

A woman sits in a room weaving a rug. It will be sold to support an organization for women. She could be killed for belonging to the organization or for weaving the rug. By chance there are two stories about this organization in the news. The phenomenon of there being two things — two of anything — has something to do with us. It's strange, the reasons there are to kill a person.

She is the character she is describing. The trick is to keep speaking in order to have responded to the interrogation. Small talk. There should always be two of something. She is the second of several things. The completion. The added on thing completes the initial entity, rounding out its possibilities — extending, even negating its potential. Finally, the entities become each other, are found to be the same or they switch positions. It's the only way we can tell we are not still in the war.

The businessman knows of the organization. Like the artist, he is in a high risk occupation. Like the women. Like us. He will say anything to the cops. He leaves clues to the falseness of his story, though in a certain way his story is precisely true. It proves that he will do whatever needs to be done, taking the situation to the next level a beat before the others in it have realized the inevitability of this step. Not like us with our small talk. Or exactly like us, like you.

Weakened by the moon

"Twin, me!" José Garcia Villa, *Aphorisms*

Why now when you are no longer
beautiful? (He said)
She works for me
Let her go
Allegory of song

"Have you written anything in the past few weeks that has become newly meaningful to you?"

"Opposed to these two positions is the experience of the poet …"
Giorgio Agamben

Apostasy
Arrival intact

Critique (She is with me)
Semblance

"What Critics call the Fable is Vision Itself" William Blake, *Vision of the Last Judgment*

Capitalism continues

43 planets around other stars and counting

Their gravity weak like ours

Having arrived in heaven alone *Ambushed by God.* Instruments are being built to spy on the universe from the moon's heaven where it is always dark.

Distance marker

She is lost in the wilderness of her work. He is unable to perceive them as different from us. Sadly there is a difference. Trust turns out to have been an inappropriate response to the situation. A faulty belief system imposes itself on the physical laws. The results are the usual ones. We watch the unfolding. It's like a wave. We are folded in it. We rest there in our work. She and you and I. It is as if we are in love. He says we are in love with capitalism and that it will shatter all of my illusions. I say I don't have illusions. Which was true then.

He is lost in his work. He sinks into it. In that way we are indistinguishable. The disconnect is the moment we work toward. The accumulation is incidental. Right. He accepts the so-called physical laws but he is a stranger in the moral universe. He has me for that. That for me.

Is this the real world? I need to see a budget. This conversation is almost unnecessary. It is not a forgivable trespass. Not if it goes as planned. You pay for your beliefs. I pay for them also. It's a physical thing.

Moon of the planet of that star

Steel yourself

From Romanticism to the Avant-garde

> "Capitalism appears unannounced."
> Karl Polanyi, *The Great Trans - formation*

Against the day of the plunge into the unknown

Closely woven rows of knots — a garden that can be carried in the hand. He wants to give her the time in the form of money but she wants it in time. The knot in thought. The garden of a thousand years with its built-in perspective. Made to be carried off. To be sold.

House plus light plus sky

A transposition problem — "Two futures coincide"<br>Norma Cole, *Coleman Hawkins Ornette Coleman*

The formal features of our relationship which has become in fact entirely business begin to overwhelm its content. We are at the cutting edge of the extremity of capital. Our designation is *Left Hand of God.*

"We had willingly entered the time stream by an exercise of the free mind ... no effort of the will power can ever lift us wholly clear of the current." John Taine, *The Time Stream*

How comfortable are you judging the madness of others?

Blinding kiss

Anthem<br>Interspersed with — Chorus of<br>Please don't<br>Aria

Urgent at the table

Not a genuine "I" thought and yet convincing though we didn't know we were ourselves at that point. She was able to help him with his trouble. "What do I have," we said, "if I don't have you?"

He is lost in the wilderness of his work. He is not aimless but driven. His being lost is not the source of the trouble. The trouble is the philosophical isolation of the cascading series of panic attacks that constitute his daily life. Light on the table in the afternoon. The leaves again. A feast of light. "I'm sorry," we said, "to fuck with you in this way." We admit "It will probably happen again."

There is a light in his eyes that says "But why not go with them into this hungry death? Go straight on to the end."

"My body had been blasted clean out of space and time. Where I had existed there was a void." Taine.

A voice

The last individual in the species

Choir

His oration

Acquire<br>
Chant<br>
Chance

The self of ecological optics

Not typical of stars

Until the wood begins to glow like the sun. I imagine being here alone and then realize I am alone. He is lost in the wilderness. But I in the music. Out behavior is criminalized. We say we are joined at the hip. That I am also lost. And the light spills over onto the floor.

"The monuments will reveal what truth there is." Eric Temple Bell, *The Time Stream*

We believed that then. He forgot to breathe. I missed the unrelieved anxiety and hostility of his laughter, the breadth of his anger. Waves of light and leaves flowed around the house like a solar wind.

"How frail is beauty's doom" Mary Robinson, "Inscribed to Maria"

Dawn from a sickly sky

| | |
|---|---|
| "inly stung" | Aria<br>Area |
| Not remembering you | Suite |

The last individual. My favorite endangered species. Reintroducing him into the wild. The problem of his trusting everyone. He is lost in the wilderness of his work. He is relentlessly alone. We share this, as we do everything though it brings us no closer, divided as we are by our language.

You and with him

Face another face

The moon burst                Like a rocket

Twin children at one time in a bookish garden. We were alone together in a small room or maybe a plane imagining the past. Unable to keep up the pretense of speaking. The words were the unreal part of the dream.

The reasonable universe                Implosion
Rock fall

The leaves and the breeze

Kissed by                This

"…self-prepared the splendid banquet stands/ Self-poured the nectar sparkles in the bowl" Mary Tighe "Psyche"  "The dead characters baffled me, and the phosphorescent decay outstripped my intellect."
John Taine, *The Time Stream*

His sun came out only at night. His work never stopped. We tied our knots and he continued in his thought. I sat with him. We talked and then sat in silence. He seemed sincere. His eyes were transparent in the light.

"Let me sing you// two yous, a shred" Taylor Brady, *Microclimates*

Two versions of what

restive but

" ... Fire won't do it/ the twin translation to another life" Gavin Selerie, "Danse Macabre"

"What did you want from me then?" he referred to a time in another city. I was traveling for a job but it was another job. "Can I touch you now?" he said from across the table. "But you already are," I said. We were an equal distance from each other. The world was a degree hotter. The equation was worked out. He was the government. I was the people. But that was then.

| | |
|---|---|
| According to his ability each | Affinity |
| | Duet |
| Not personal but human | Like breasts |

Through him like an accordian

Vatic trajectory *Song For* sung for

Mechanical breath

The planet dark around us. Hungry for our missed tea but unwilling to leave. All day waiting to speak. Constructing the afternoon around his stylized anger. "No ray of light falls on the darkness of your heart." Andrew Bird, "Pathetique" A banquet of possibility is spread out before us. Is physical. Is imminent or is already taking place.

The pattern is suspended around the woman creating it. She is involved in a conspiracy. The pattern is traditional. It is over her head. She has hung it there. Information is dense in the material. She can project the future with this form. Her method is not relational, though she exists in a complex fabric of social relationships, but is more interruptive.

I feel the music inside me

But the world is a threat

"Western *I*. Casting unecological shadow." Gail Scott, *My Paris*

He is lost in the music of his work. We are the largest consuming nation. We have to work out a future. You and me and I. A next step in our dance of death. He called his friends Deaths. Part of the burden of the past now electronically sloughed off.

The woman feels the sand in her hands. In her veins. The organization is warm against her skin and under her feet. There is a roar from a vent by her window where the whole city breathes. She tells herself to enjoy her exhaustion. People are imprisoned. In themselves. She is alive.

Does he support the organization? What is this business we are in together? These and other questions when we meet. Our connections strained beyond recognition. He is lost in the wilderness of his work. "Hard-won, self-acquired, self-earned property!" Karl Marx, *Das Kapital.* Our small talk deteriorates into chaos like an ecosystem about to tip.

"But what is supposed to rise from this collapse? Only their original, intimate dialogue." Brent Cunningham, *Bird & Forest*

His face is my face. Or mine is hers. It is a wholesale use of one by the other. There are objections. "It is important," she says "to get used to the hunger." She is my twin as much as she is yours. Mine is the name of the moon in that system. The trajectories are interlocked. Our exchange is also lopsided. Like a cosmic event, it has the unevenness of personal talk.

Like statues the women are destroyed. They break. We break down. Into.

Dirge
The rocks
You taught
The disbelief

Our birthday again. Everything we can speak is between us all the time especially now. As I stand and you list. Your hard-won status as a dead poet is history but is not the only historical thing. "These knots you taught" and the portable aspects of what we do remain when there is no speech.

"Twin heads now lean, recontort." John Wilkinson, *Speaking Twins.* Finding out late about the third twin who will change everything. An electronic song or code book sequence unravels our activity. Will the new configuration protect them? Us. Me. Zealous soldier of. All that we are. In all our twinned glory. Fortune. From what will.

Be known

Embattled ecstatic

<table>
<tr><td></td><td>Aporia<br>Our community</td></tr>
<tr><td>Subcontracted</td><td>Villification</td></tr>
<tr><td>Testimonial</td><td>Not</td></tr>
</table>

Last man standing

"The head and legs of the Buddha"

It's true she was the center of it then. The big lake of her face. Her words dying. The just outside of town thing. What used to be called a trip breaks down. The organization is in trouble. The landscape takes itself apart. Like a shot. Fast. Another old world word. Onward.

Into the valley of

Face to the wall

The war

That image destroyed

## Last Song

Packing again
This much no more

That move you made
Back then

A line of men
A man's line

No retreat
Stone by stone

My gun is your gun
Your mind

The orange light
Falling though the window

On the avenue
Me and my nemesis

That face. Those things. To think that there were two of them. Two of us. Your triumph awash with light. Telltale sign. The explosion. Lack of luck. Emerged from the meeting barely alive.

Into the valley of death
The last song

The sky in the future
You have no fate

Wild blue
Canon loose

Gorge rising
Was that you?

## Pure Lyric

Like pure war a politics and architecture. The ramparts are built to be destroyed. Arriving at another city the city remembered before us is just a name. The politics of working together. Of writing together including movement. Logistics. Only the form of our existence is left like a retinal pattern. An engagement. A list of our accomplishments composed of these notes coheres for a moment in local space.

There is an individual. Nobody helps him but nobody talks about it. The beds of the hotels when we were that lucky. Not a competition though someone wins. He uses me like he uses the other equipment. Simple repetition. I can't say what I would do. Or did. Or know.

## My Geography

Who walks with you?
A walk is given to oneself
To the sea an enclosure
Lake or bay with a shore
The immediate sea
Self-exposure on one side
Lake shore divide
Tunneling [        ]
Takes off lost
Series of blocks
Who goes out into

## Arrhythmia

You and you again go
Returning as you do
Known or unknown
A thought as in temporal
Eternal as turning
Step away from the car

Both of us agree to be
You define yourself as
Named and as speaking
But what not said was
A pause in:
A soft schedule

Not calendarized
But frozen outside a miniature
But central ocean
Deepest lake
Survival means going
Mistaken as with any sudden
Forward jerk

I created myself to death
That said
Dying words
Wasn't in fact

What she said was
The next thought we walk
In our own blood

## I Have You

I don't need the sea
Your bitter repetition
City open like a wound
To the sea
Although my life is sad
You tell me the time in time
But slowed way down

In my pages also torn
Sleep again then sleep
Where are you going
In this drowned world?

I have
Said my life
Audio this morning streaming
Born on the beach of the lake
A need to see the river
To the sea

# Transformation of the Twins

Not going back
"something passes between two things … "
Hospital or moon
Forget the moon
"to feel oneself in heaven"
I have to go now
Gone along the edge road with
She as me in far off
Daily apocalypse but no judgment
No judgment but in
As if already done
But it was not like hell
An engraving
Together again before
The funeral before the war
Then I am the man
In this lake or womblike
Neighborhood of us
Two hungers enlarged
Unless and until
Ordinary hunger
You feed me with yourself

## No Moon

Old time synthesizer
Emotion ocean

Lean on the dial
Acoustic sunrise

Radio and sky the same claim
The same way back

Recorded laughter call-in host
Bubbling through the stratosphere

From your veins in blue trails
To your brain and back

Never going off duty claims
A direct channel

Fake moon
Nonunique finite and faithful

Animate schematic universe
Smart jump

At no time does it get better
Death and development

Our other new department
Existing fragmentation

Thinking-in-time
Visible all night

## My Scream

Today I am screaming in love
The water created by raining
For him to steal me and say
I have a song for your lovely street

The lavender moon where you want it to be
The water created by chiming
Strings in a circular pattern like rings
Like pebbles off the dock at the end of air

This will fall away you say
Today screaming in love I am
Not present but presence only naturally
Using something other than your name

To mean you in one word
Reflexively and before the end
Of the song we sing when we
On the street again with your lovely I have

To steel myself when people talk
It is as if they are singing
Why do you rise in your purple thing?
What is it that a moon can mean?

Not round but straight
Not soft but soft what moon now
With its light me after all this
Mere heat entering my heart

Who do you love and what
Do you know about that sweet anything
You are not telling me repetition
I don't already know?